JUL 2 5 201

P9-CWD-527

J 398.469
Gui

Dragons

BLOOMINGDALE PUBLIC LIBRARY
101 FAIRFIELD WAY
BLOOMINGDALE, IL 60108
630 - 529 - 3120

Charlotte Guillain

Raintree
Chicago, Illinois

www.heinemannraintree.com
Visit our website to find out more information about Heinemann-Raintree books.

To order:
☎ Phone 888-454-2279
🖥 Visit www.heinemannraintree.com to browse our catalog and order online.

© 2011 Raintree
an imprint of Capstone Global Library, LLC
Chicago, Illinois

All rights reserved. No part of this publication may be reproduced or transmitted in any form or by any means, electronic or mechanical, including photocopying, recording, taping, or any information storage and retrieval system, without permission in writing from the publisher.

Edited by Adrian Vigliano, Rebecca Rissman, and Nancy Dickmann
Designed by Joanna Hinton Malivoire
Levelling by Jeanne Clidas
Original illustrations by Christian Slade
Picture research by Elizabeth Alexander
Production by Victoria Fitzgerald

Printed and bound in China by CTPS

14 13 12 11 10
10 9 8 7 6 5 4 3 2 1

Library of Congress Cataloging-in-Publication Data
Guillain, Charlotte.
   Dragons / Charlotte Guillain.
      p. cm.—(Mythical creatures)
   Includes bibliographical references and index.
   ISBN 978-1-4109-3804-6 (hc)—ISBN 978-1-4109-3811-4 (pb)   1. Dragons—Juvenile literature.   I. Title.
   GR830.D7G85 2011
   398'.469—dc22   2009052419

Acknowledgments
The author and publishers are grateful to the following for permission to reproduce copyright material: Alamy pp. **8** (© Photos 12), **17** (© INTERFOTO), **21** (© Chris Howarth/Argentina), **24** (© Bill Bachman); Corbis pp. **15** (© So Hing-Keung), **28** (© Theo Allofs); Getty Images p. **18** (Redferns); Photolibrary pp. **14** (Larry Dale Gordon/Pacific Stock), **22** (Silvio Fiore/Superstock), **25** (JOE MC DONALD/Animals Animals); Shutterstock pp. **9** (© Taily), **10** (© erom), **11** (© juliengrondin), **12** (© Sergey Mikhaylov), **19** (© Lance Bellers), **29** (© Linda Bucklin).

Every effort has been made to contact copyright holders of any material reproduced in this book. Any omissions will be rectified in subsequent printings if notice is given to the publisher.

Disclaimer
All the Internet addresses (URLs) given in this book were valid at the time of going to press. However, due to the dynamic nature of the Internet, some addresses may have changed, or sites may have changed or ceased to exist since publication. While the author and publisher regret any inconvenience this may cause readers, no responsibility for any such changes can be accepted by either the author or the publisher.

Some words are shown in bold, **like this**. You can find out what they mean by looking in the glossary.

Contents

What Is a Mythical Creature?

Stories around the world tell us about strange creatures, such as werewolves and fairies. For many years people have wondered if these **mythical** creatures really exist. What do you think?

DID YOU KNOW?
People tell vampire stories in Europe, Africa, Asia, Australia, and South America.

Have you heard stories about mermaids? Do you think they could exist?

What Is a Dragon?

Myths from around the world tell us about dragons. These huge monsters are shown in many paintings. They often look like giant lizards or crocodiles.

DID YOU KNOW?

The Thai Dragon is a very hot chili pepper used in Asian cooking. When people eat the pepper it feels as if they are breathing fire!

The dragons in many stories breathe fire. Other dragons fly high in the air. Some **myths** tell us that dragon blood is like a magic medicine.

DID YOU KNOW?
In some places people believed dragons could control the rain.

The Dragon Myth

crocodile

Myths about dragons began thousands of years ago. There are stories about dragons in the **Bible**, Greek myths, and other old **legends**. Why did so many people believe in dragons?

Where did the dragon myth come from?

Did people think:

- lizards, alligators, crocodiles, or snakes were dragons?

- lightning in the sky was a dragon breathing fire?

- a volcano erupting was a dragon roaring?

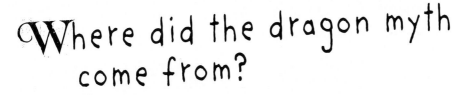

volcano

Dragons of China

Dragons have been important in China for thousands of years. Chinese people believed dragons could be friendly and would bring them good luck.

China

DID YOU KNOW?
Every twelve years in China it is the Year of the Dragon. People born in this year are supposed to have good luck and a long life.

Chinese dragons weren't always helpful. Some stories tell us how dragons got angry when humans didn't **respect** them. Then they would stop the rain or bring floods.

DID YOU KNOW?
People in China did dragon dances and raced dragon boats to keep the dragons happy.

15

Dragons of Europe

Dragons in Europe were fierce monsters. Many people thought they were giant winged snakes living in underground caves. Many stories told of dragons burning down villages and taking young women away.

England

Wales

Europe

DID YOU KNOW?

People believed that dragons guarded treasure. **Knights** would try to kill a dragon and take its treasure.

17

Many famous **legends** tell of heroes fighting dragons. An old English poem is about the hero named Beowulf (say *bay-oh-wolf*) fighting a snake-like dragon. Another story tells us that Saint George killed a dragon and rescued a princess.

Saint George

DID YOU KNOW?

People in Wales, United Kingdom have a red dragon on their flag. An old Welsh story is about a red dragon fighting and killing a white dragon that **invaded** Wales.

American Dragons

People also tell dragon **myths** in North and South America. In Central America there is a myth about the dragon god Chac (say *chock*). He controlled the water so people gave him gifts for rain.

North America

Colombia

Central America

South America

20

DID YOU KNOW?

In Colombia people believed in a goddess called Bachue (say *bash-oo-ey*). They thought she **created** humans and then turned herself and her husband into dragons.

This is a statue of another South American dragon goddess.

Dragons of the Middle East

In the Middle East, there are many stories about dragons. In Babylon people talked about a scaly dragon called the sirrush (say *ser-RUSH*). This dragon had back legs like an eagle. In Sumeria people believed in a snake-like dragon called Kur. Babylon and Sumeria were where Iraq is now.

ancient Sumerian temple

DID YOU KNOW?
People believed
the sirrush had a
long neck and a
horn on its head.
It also had a
forked tongue.

Middle East

Iraq

Close Relatives

There are other creatures in **myths** that are similar to dragons. Myths from Europe tell about a reptile like a snake with two legs and wings called a wyvern (say *why-vurn*).

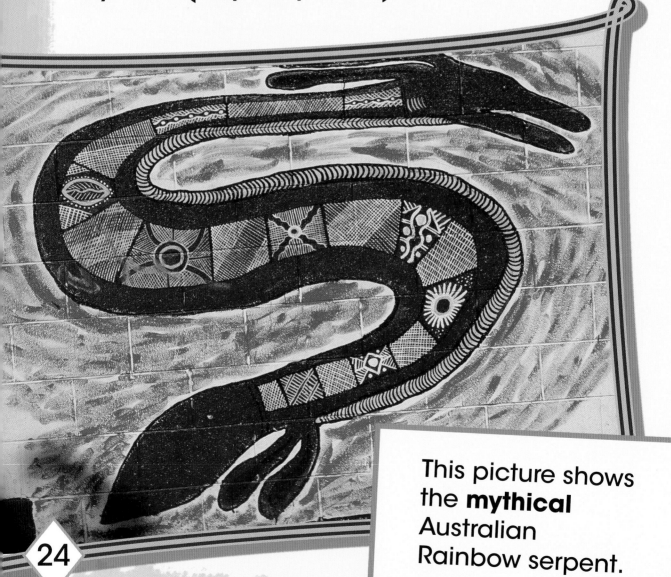

This picture shows the **mythical** Australian Rainbow serpent.

DID YOU KNOW?

Some people believed in a monster called a basilisk (say *bass-ill-isk*). A real basilisk is a lizard that can run across water!

Could Dragons Exist?

What do you think?

 They could be real...

- People all over the world tell stories about dragons.

 I'm not so sure...

- You can't believe all the stories you hear. Lots of stories around the world are similar.

 They could be real...

- Dragons could be hiding deep in mountain caves.

 I'm not so sure...

- Dragons are supposed to be so big that surely we would have seen one.

They could be real...

- We now know dinosaurs used to live on Earth. Maybe dragons did too.

 I'm not so sure...

- Scientists have found remains of dinosaurs. They haven't found any **evidence** of dragons.

The truth is that dragons don't really exist. But they make a great story!

Reality Versus Myth

Komodo dragon (real)

Found: Indonesia

Lives: On hot, dry islands

Eats: Birds, small animals, baby Komodo dragons

Seen: Young Komodo dragons can hide in trees, older ones dig holes in the shade to rest

Special power: Has a poisonous bite

Dragon (myth)

Found: All over the world

Lives: Deep in caves underground or in pools of water

Eats: People

Seen: Only in paintings and in the movies!

Special power: Magic

Glossary

Bible special book in the Christian religion

create to make something out of nothing, by using powers or magic

evidence facts that tell us whether something is true

invade to attack

knight a kind of historical fighter. Knights often wore armor and rode horses.

legend traditional story that may or may not be true

myth traditional story, often about magical creatures and events

mythical found in myths

respect to treat someone politely and properly

Find Out More

Books

Carrel, Douglas and Steer, Dugald. *Dragonology: The Complete Book of Dragons*. Cambridge, MA: Candlewick Press, 2003.

Doeden, Matt. *Dragonatomy*. Mankato, MN: Capstone Press, 2008.

Peffer, Jessica. *DragonArt: How to Draw Fantastic Dragons and Fantasy Creatures*. Iola, WI: IMPACT Books, 2005.

Websites

www.nationalgallery.org.uk/paintings/paolo-uccello-saint-george-and-the-dragon
Paolo Ucello's painting of Saint George and the dragon is on the British National Gallery Website.

http://pbskids.org/dragontales/index_sw.html
This Website is full of games and activities that are all about dragons!

Index

32

3 1531 00378 5042